SOVIET MILITARY BADGES

A History and Collector's Guide

Richard Hollingdale

First published 2016

Amberley Publishing
The Hill, Stroud
Gloucestershire, GL5 4EP

www.amberley-books.com

Copyright © Richard Hollingdale, 2016

The right of Richard Hollingdale to be identified as the Author of this work has been asserted in accordance with the Copyrights, Designs and Patents Act 1988.

ISBN 978 1 4456 4916 0 (print)
ISBN 978 1 4456 4917 7 (ebook)

All rights reserved. No part of this book may be reprinted or reproduced or utilised in any form or by any electronic, mechanical or other means, now known or hereafter invented, including photocopying and recording, or in any information storage or retrieval system, without the permission in writing from the Publishers.

British Library Cataloguing in Publication Data.
A catalogue record for this book is available from the British Library.

Typesetting by Amberley Publishing.
Printed in the UK.

Contents

Introduction	5
Sports Badges	7
Excellence Badges	16
Youth Membership Pins	27
Guards Badges	31
Military Proficiency Badges	36
Parachute Badges	40
Extended Service Clasps	49
Officer Academy Graduation Badges	52
Military Schools	54
Military Colleges	56
Higher Academies	58
Technical Clasps	64
Celebration Badges	79
Miscellaneous Military Badges	89
Note About the Prescribed Order of Wear	92

Introduction

Why 1946 and Not Before?

The aim of this book has been to offer the reader the greatest amount of information in the most readily accessible format – a pocket reference work that can easily be dipped into in order to help the reader quickly identify the badges in their collections, or make them aware of other variations yet to be found. In order to achieve this aim it has been necessary to divide the Soviet period into two main eras: Revolution through to Great Patriotic War (1918–1945), and the Cold War (1946–1991). This divide has also been necessary because of the wealth of material produced by the USSR in all of its eighty-three years (a book of this size could not adequately cover such a long period of time). Similarly, a distinction has been drawn between the pre-1945 and post-1945 badges because the late 1940s witnessed a material shift in the appearance and culture of Soviet badges. This shift was a reflection of a changing military – the Red Army was renamed the Soviet Army, which, in the shadow of the atomic bomb, developed a whole new defence strategy – and so created a notable difference in the design of the post-war badges when compared to any of their Red Army predecessors. The time distinction also denotes a bias in the interests of the author, who has always had a greater interest in Cold War Soviet history and accepts that anything which predates that time period would be better left to a different historian.

As far as possible, an example of every military badge from the chosen era has been featured. Where this goal has not been fulfilled (in the form of an archive photograph or colour plate), the text will offer a description or an indication that more varieties exist. It would have been nice to have included many more images of Soviet Navy badges (a particular favourite of the author, which exist in such abundance that they could fill a book of their own), but the arrival of reproductions has meant that a significant portion of this study has been applied to the reverse of the featured badges. At the time of writing, the extent of reproductions on the 1946–91 market is not too pronounced, but this can only change for the worse if the pattern of earlier periods is taken into consideration. With this in mind, a small amount of space has been given over to the badges' prescribed order of wear as forgers often try to authenticate a uniform by applying (what they think) are applicable badges, or help make badges look more valuable by grouping them together and claiming that they were once the property of one recipient. In order to do this, though, some other points are not included. Alternatively, it could be that a badge is not mentioned because the author is unaware of it. After more than twenty years of study such an oversight is believed to be unlikely, but in the event that it has happened an advanced apology is made. Certainly, correspondence with readers is encouraged via the publishers and if something has been missed out the author would appreciate his attention being brought to the missing piece.

A final introductory note needs to be said about the badges in relation to their material value as it is a feature of collecting that most commonly determines availability on the market and attractiveness to collectors. Many of the badges featured in this book are still readily obtainable, which is unfortunate for those who appreciate this slice of history as the seeming abundance has left post-war Soviet military badges largely overlooked. This is because large armies – and there was none bigger than the Soviet Army in its day – can have the habit of making it look as though certain awards were 'handed out with the rations', but that is rarely the case. Among its other aims, this study seeks to highlight not so much the material value but the merit value of the badges and so cultivate a greater appreciation and respect for them. In a practical sense, it will also draw attention to the large number of variations that sometimes existed and so an understanding that, although a certain badge could be seen as collectively quite common, some rarities are hidden alongside them and so deserving of a second look. As the photographs that accompany this short introduction demonstrate, even the most common badges were not necessarily commonly awarded. The photographs also serve to remind us that these badges are the record of people's lives and that something we might dismiss as common and worthless was, in its time, a true distinction that had been long trained for.

Every attempt has been made to seek permission for copyright material used in this book. However, if material has been inadvertently used without permission/acknowledgement the author apologises and stresses that the publishers will make any necessary corrections at the first opportunity. On occasion it has been necessary to include the badges of the other Eastern Bloc nations. When this has occurred it has been to serve as a comparison in order to help collectors avoid buying non-Soviet badges by mistake (dealers in military antiques – let us avoid calling them experts – cannot be relied upon to know where their stock has originated from). For those who are also interested in the badges of the Eastern Bloc readers are directed to an earlier publication by the same author, *Warsaw Pact Badges*.

Soviet transport troops from the 1950s demonstrating the general scarcity of awards. The awards that can be seen are youth pins, sports badges and, in one case, Excellent Driver (top row, centre).

Sports Badges

Civilian and Paramilitary Sports Badges

Within any totalitarian state there is often an indistinct line between the military and civil authorities. The USSR was no exception and there was a wealth of patriotic clubs and societies engineered with which to ensure the health, loyalty, and support of the people. Out of these organisations, the most significant to this study was the GTO, Ready for Work and Defence. It organised physical education and sports events which culminated in a variety of awards for the participants (many of which were issued as badges that were worn on the uniforms of serving military personnel).

As with all of the other classes and groups of badges featured within this book, the GTO sports badges progressed through a variety of changes due to variations in design, materials and manufacturer. The first examples featured date from 1946 to 1961. Quite a wide range had, in fact, existed since the 1930s, but only the 1946 Type seems to have been worn by military personnel during the period covered by this book. From 1961 to 1972 an alternative design replaced the 1946 type, although the new

1946–61 First Category GTO Sports badges.

1946–61 First Category GTO Sports badges.
Reverse showing screw post and pin attachment.

badges were still rendered in high-quality gilt brass and enamel. As demonstrated in the accompanying illustrations, several variations existed due to subtle differences in design or manufacturer. The most obvious difference was the changed position of the runner's right arm, which was more pronounced in the earlier versions. After 1972 the same range of badges were kept with the only difference that they were made of painted aluminium.

Other sporting distinctions commonly encountered on military uniforms were the five Sports Category badges. The first three awards were numbered Categories Three, Two and One. Categories Three and Two had a standard design which featured a man running and the relevant award number. In addition to the category number, the two classes were colour coded: green for Third Category, blue for Second Category. Category One badges were red in colour and featured a small picture of the sport at which the recipient excelled. The total variety of Category One badges in existence is not known as the range of sports celebrated, within this author's experience, started with chess and ended with parachuting, but had anything from figure skating and

1961–72 GTO Sports badges, alternating, early and later issue enamel versions.

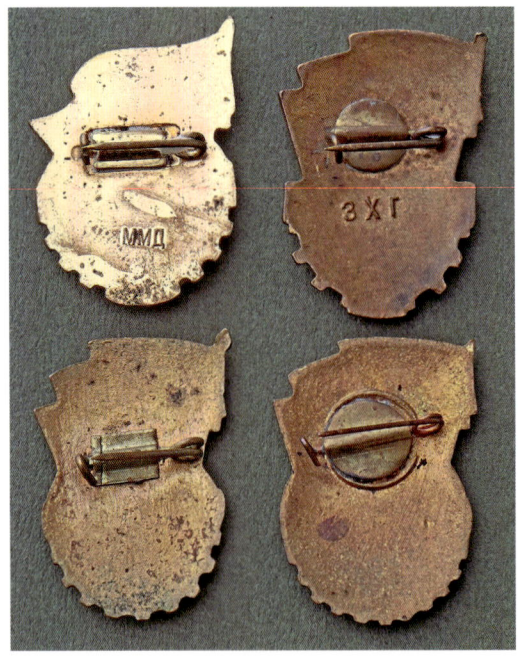

1961–72 GTO Sports badges. Reverse showing variations in pin design and maker's marks.

motor racing through to boxing and football in between. Beyond the Category One badge was the Candidate Master of Sport and then Master of Sport. The latter badge was of significant importance for each one to have been engraved with an issue number. Such numbers run into the millions, but, nonetheless, the Master of Sport badge is still one of the most collectable non-military post-war Soviet badges. All of the category sports badges started off being issued in gilt brass and enamel and, with the exception of the Master of Sport, was soon issued in painted aluminium. It is assumed that the enamelled versions of the junior category badges were short-lived as they are significantly scarcer than their cheaper counterparts. Somewhat less common are the sports parachute badges issued by the DOSAAF, Paramilitary Sports Association. These were first awarded in the 1940s as high-quality gilt brass and enamel and came in three classes: First, Second and Third – indicated by a number in the centre of the badge. The badge could be awarded a multiple of times and so many had a small pendant beneath with the additional number of times it had been awarded recorded upon it. As with the GTO and Sports Category badges, these Sports Parachute badges were later issued in painted aluminium.

Sports Instructor badges, left to right: early gilt and enamel type with later painted aluminium.

Clockwise: Master of Sport, Early Type Sports Instructor, First Type Category One Sports badge in brass and enamels.

Selection of youth sport pins.

Sport Category badges, left to right: Class Three, Class Two, Class One, Candidate for Master of Sport, Master of Sport.

Sport Category Class One, top left clockwise: early gilt and enamel type plus various painted aluminium versions.

Master of Sport.

Sports Badges

Category Sports badges, left to right: First Type gilt and enamel with later painted aluminium.

Sports Category badges, left to right: Classes Three and Two featuring an alternative design.

Later Type Sports Parachute badges, c. 1960s onwards.

DOSAAF (Paramilitary Sports Association) Good Service award.

Military Sports Badges

The first officially designated military sports badges date from 1966. Prior to that date one other category possibly existed, although their military status is not universally agreed upon by collectors. It is possible that these pre-1966 badges were initially civilian awards that were later adopted by the military, as was the case with the Excellence in Physical Culture award. What makes this hypothesis seem likely is that these badges are found celebrating proficiency in a variety of competitive sports (just like the Category Sports badges), but only those featuring a man running seem to be seen on the uniforms of actively serving military personnel – lending suspicion to the thought that they were exclusively for the military. Whatever the case, these debated badges date from the 1950s and were a common feature on the uniforms of many service personnel until the mid-1960s, whereupon they appear to have been replaced by the 1966 Type (which lends further support to the idea that they were of a military status). As with the GTO badges, these circular sports badges came in three classes: First, Second and Third. Similarly to the GTO sports badges the numerical class was also indicated by the badge's colour: red for First Class, blue for Second Class, and green for Third Class. The vast majority were fitted with a screw post, although some examples had a pin attachment. Probably indicating a difference in age, two types of manufacture are observed: a two-piece construction and a one-piece construction. The only known examples observed by the author were all rendered in gilt brass and enamel, which suggests that this class of badge was discontinued before 1964 (the point at which the USSR started to introduce painted aluminium badges). The 1966 Type Military Sports badges themselves followed the well-established system of classes and colour-coding. A screw post attachment seems to have been the most common, although versions with a pin attachment were also issued. Due to the date of its first

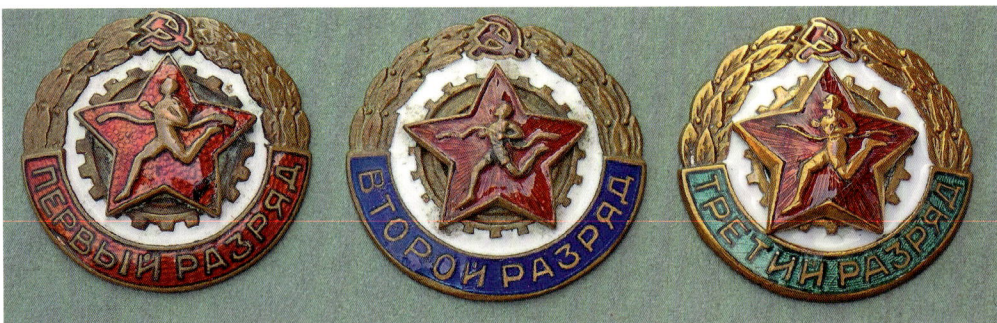

Above: 1950s sports badges, left to right: First, Second and Third Classes.

Left: Reverse 1950s sports badges, left to right: two-piece construction and one-piece.

Soviet sailor from the 1950s wearing one of the circular sports badges which predated the 1966 Type Military Sports badges.

Above: 1966–94 Military Sports badges Classes One, Two and Three.

Right: Reverse 1966–94 Military Sports badges demonstrating various makers and design variations. A solid-backed pin variety can also be found.

Soviet officer cadet wearing one of the 1966 Type Military Sports badges. Of all the badges featured in this book, the 1966 Military Sports badge is the most common.

issue and the relatively low status it enjoyed, the 1966 Type Military Sports badge was only ever manufactured in painted aluminium. Without featuring any overtly political insignia, this particular badge was not retired from service until 1994 (outlasting the USSR by three years and the Soviet Army by one year).

Other notable sports badges were the Military Competition Sports Badge and the aforementioned Excellence in Physical Culture. As previously stated, the Excellence in Physical Culture started off as a civilian award and only later gained military acceptance. It was introduced *c.* 1947 as a high-grade two-piece gilt and enamel badge, sufficiently prestigious enough to be given an issue number on the reverse. It remained in service until the end of the USSR, but was later made of painted aluminium (although it remained a two-piece construction and continued to be issued with an engraved serial number). As a consequence, the Excellence in Physical Culture ranks alongside the Master of Sport as one of the most collectable badges of its type. In contrast, the Military Competition Sports badge appears to have only been manufactured in painted aluminium and, although it was positioned on the uniform above other military breast badges, it appears to have occupied a fairly modest status. Of greater interest to the collector are the Military Competition badges awarded by individual services (e.g. air force) for individual events such as shooting contests. The only thing that can be said of them here in the given space is that they were numerous in design and thus individually rare. Equally, as a category of badge they were also rare when compared to the generic sports badges described above and so are now highly collectable.

Left to right: later type Excellence in Physical Culture badge, Military Sports Competition badge.

Sports Badges 15

Reverse later type Excellence in Physical Culture award.

Air Force Sports Competition badge.

Reverse Air Force Sports Competition badge.

Excellence Badges

Army, Navy and Air Force

Excellence badges were first introduced in 1942. Their aim was to help rebuild the quality and confidence of the average Red Army soldier after the crushing defeats of the previous year. Initially these badges celebrated military excellence within the ten core branches of the armed forces – e.g. Excellent Infantry, Excellent Artillery and Excellent Tanker – but eventually covered almost every possible trade from Excellent Torpedo Handler to Excellent Army Baker. In all, twenty-three different trades or branches of service were celebrated in the form of an Excellence badge. The very last of the Great Patriotic War excellence badges was the Excellent Airman, instituted in 1950. Other than its rather late arrival, it was also noteworthy in that it sported one of two designs: early and later types. The early type had the legend Excellent Airman evenly spaced above and below the central device (the classic hammer and sickle emblem of the USSR), whereas the later type had the same legend contained within the upper portion of the badge. All other excellence badges appear to have retained the same design, although variations in manufacture were observed over time, resulting in a progressively flatter profile. In every case but one, the wartime excellence badges were only ever produced in gilt brass and enamel as they were discontinued before the adoption of painted aluminium. The only exception was the Excellent Firefighter, which varied from the other badges in two ways: earlier examples were a two-piece construction, and the final version was rendered in painted aluminium as it was the only skill-specific Excellence badge to be retained beyond the 1950s. Of all the badges covered by this study, the wartime excellence badges are the most heavily reproduced. Most of the reproductions are quite easy to detect, they have a chemically darkened patina which is too evenly applied to fool anyone in particular, but the quality and accuracy is improving. It would be nice to offer some detailed advice, but from the personal experience of this author (who bought collector's guides from other periods and still ended up buying reproductions), the best thing to do is to study known originals as much as possible. There is no substitute for the personal study and handling of originals. For those who do not have access to original badges the collector's website collectrussia.com is strongly recommended due to the quality of its merchandise, photography and accompanying notes.

Towards the end of the 1950s, 1959 being a commonly quoted year, the skill-specific Excellence badges were replaced by three Unified Excellence badges. These celebrated military excellence in the army, navy and air force, which remained in service until 1991 (whereupon the national armies of the former Soviet states replaced them with their own versions). As with most other badges of this era, the Unified Excellence badges came in two basic types: early, brass and enamel construction, and later, painted aluminium. The First Type Unified Excellence badges were often subjected to one of two types of military fashion. In the first case, it seems to have been common for soldiers to have removed the dark grey-blue painted border from the outer edge of the badge. On occasion, this has been seen as evidence of an earlier type, but all examples lacking a painted border (as have been observed by this author) have shown evidence of traces

1950 Excellent Airman badge. Last of the Second World War-style excellence badges to be introduced.

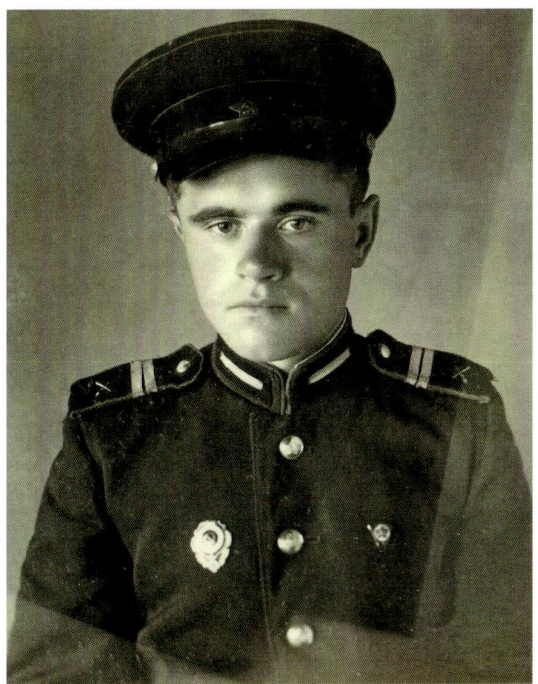

Soviet artilleryman photographed in the 1950s wearing the Excellent Artillery badge. Of interest, he also wears the First Type Komsomol pin.

of paint and/or minute scratch marks. The second alteration, which appears to have been practised by navy personnel alone, was to apply a white painted border. In both cases, the lack of a border or the application of white paint does not indicate any level of additional rarity or collectability. Some of the First Type Unified Excellence badges are found with a screw post attachment to the rear. Inspection of such badges has demonstrated evidence of alteration and it seems most likely that this class of badge was always manufactured with a pin attachment. The Type Two painted aluminium Unified Excellence badges were introduced in the 1970s. Variations in design on the obverse side of the badges appears to have been non-existent, although the reverse sides often prove to be quite varied as a result of having been made by different manufacturers. Not in any sense can it be said that either the Type One or Type Two Unified Excellence badges rare – all are very common – yet the earlier type is still being reproduced.

Left to right: First Type Unified Excellence badge for army and navy without painted border.

Reverse First Type Unified Excellence badge.

Excellence Badges

Close-up of maker's mark on First Type Unified Excellence badge.

First Type Unified Excellence badges for, left to right: army, air force, navy.

Left to right: last issue Excellent Military Firefighter, Excellent Army, Air Force, Navy.

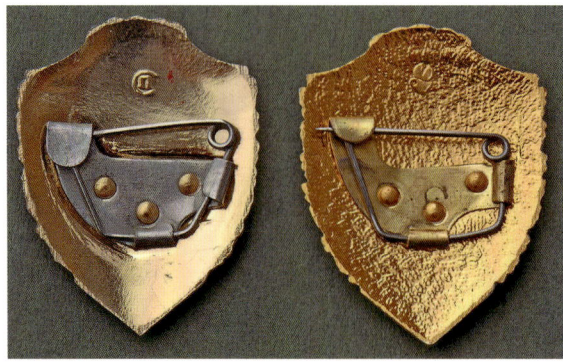

Reverse late issue Unified Excellence badges demonstrating variations in design and manufacturer.

Soviet sailor photographed in the 1960s wearing the unified Excellent Navy badge with the addition of an unofficial white border.

Soviet airman wearing the unified Excellent Air Force badge in 1971. He also wears a Military Proficiency badge, Class One; 1966 Type Military Sports badge, and Category Two civilian sports badge.

Frontier Guards

When studying the excellence badges of the USSR within a military context, it is worth looking at those of the Frontier Guard. The reasons for including the Frontier Guard are several fold: the Soviet Army and Frontier Guard shared much the same uniform and insignia, fulfilled many of the same functions and duties (including armed combat), and qualified for many of the same awards. For the most part, between 1945 and 1991 the Frontier Guard actually saw more active service than the Soviet armed forces, and so are deserving of a mention in that respect also. The one area where the Frontier Guard did differ from the Soviet armed forces was the range of excellence badges made available to them. As demonstrated by one of the archive photographs, Frontier Guards could qualify for the Army Unified Excellence badge, but this appears to have been more of an exception than anything else. For most Frontier Guards the reward for excellence was to receive a badge unique to their branch of service. The first Frontier Guard excellence badge relevant to this study was issued between 1953 and 1957. It came in two forms: standard one-piece construction, and a significantly rarer three-piece construction.

These badges were replaced in 1957 by a near identical badge except for a few small differences (the most notable of which was the removal of the Cyrillic initials KGB from the front of the badge, other changes were due to variations in construction). In 1964 the first of the painted aluminium badges came into existence. Interestingly, the change in the method of construction was also matched by a slight change in design; the badge was made smaller and the guard featured wore a summer (as opposed to winter) uniform and faced in the opposite direction. The final version introduced in the 1970s was increased in size, and abandoned a gold finish in favour of silver. It came in two versions: slightly rarer variant with a green border, and a more common version without painted border. When compared to the Unified Excellence badges awarded by the Soviet armed forces those issued to the Frontier Guard are noticeably rarer, although not so much so that they should be considered within themselves as being particularly scarce.

Excellent Frontier Guard, 1957–64 Type.

Left to right: Excellent Frontier Guard 1964–70s, 1970s–1991, later issue Internal Army (armed police and factory guards).

Reverse, left to right: Excellent Airman, Frontier Guard 1957–64, last issue Firefighter.

Reverse Excellent Frontier Guard 1964–70s, 1970s–91, later issue Internal Army.

Soviet Frontier Guard photographed between 1966 and 1968 wearing the first of the painted aluminium Excellent Frontier Guard badges. He also wears one of the 1966 Type Military sports badges.

Two Soviet frontier guards photographed in 1981. The near-most man wears both the Excellent Army and Excellent Frontier Guard badges. Both men wear the Second Type Komsomol youth pin.

Miscellaneous Excellence badges

The story of the Excellence badge does not quite stop at the Frontier Guard as several other military badges can also be classed (if only tentatively at times) as being an Excellence badge. The most commonly encountered of these is the Excellent Military Construction. In came in two versions: early and later. The early version, issued from the 1960s, was made of gilt brass and enamel with a screw post attachment to the rear. The later version, issued from the 1970s onwards, was of a near identical design and construction. The only difference was that the crossed grenade and submachine gun at the base of the badge was in high relief on the earlier type and in low relief on the later type. The earlier type can be considered as being less common to scarce, whereas the later type is unquestionably common. Unlike many other badges of the same era, the Excellent Military Construction badge does not appear to have been produced in painted aluminium. Presumably, construction troops of the air force qualified for the same badge (as often they did with other types of award), but the Soviet Navy retained the distinction of having its own military construction badge. The Excellent Naval Military Construction badge was much the same in size and quality to those issued to the army except it featured images of a naval flavour (most notably the inclusion of an anchor). As with many other badges exclusive to the Soviet Navy, these examples are much rarer than their army counterparts and should be considered as quite scarce and so highly collectable. The reason for this is due to the relatively small size of the Soviet Navy when compared to the Soviet Army. The USSR had always seen itself as a land empire (understandable when its vast borders were taken into consideration, coupled with the fact that the USSR lacked a large-sized port that remained free of ice during the winter) and so the navy remained small. Only in the 1970s did the Soviet Navy expand to a size that was more in keeping with that of the army. As a consequence Soviet Navy badges that predate the 1970s are generally scarce if not rare.

On occasion individual military districts could award their own excellence badges. The two featured are both from the 1980s, but still managed to successfully demonstrate the sizeable variations in design and manufacture that did exist between them.

Entertainment and creative expression were an important part of a Soviet soldier's life as the High Command was keenly aware that a bored soldier was a potentially dangerous thing. A lot of attention, therefore, was paid to creative and artistic endeavours, the summit of which was the awarding of the Excellence in Cultural Achievement. Unlike other Excellence badges, the Excellence in Cultural Achievement came in the form of a pendant suspended from a bar and was individually numbered. In keeping with almost all other badges of the era, though, the Excellence in Cultural Achievement was first produced in gilt brass and enamel and then painted aluminium.

Left to right: Excellent Military Construction First Type, Naval Military Construction, Excellent Military Construction later issue.

Reverse Excellent Construction badges, left to right: early issue army, navy, later issue army.

Excellence badges awarded by military districts, left to right: Baltic Excellent Guard Duty, Turkmenistan.

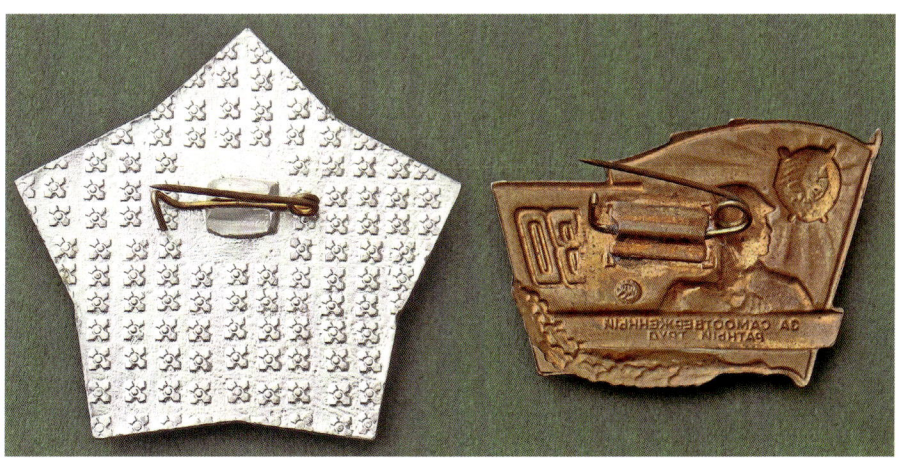

Reverse regional military district excellence badges.

The last badges to be mentioned in this chapter were for mine clearance. They were not excellence badges in the strictest sense (arguably, in some ways, more commemorative celebration badges), but without a certain level of excellence having been achieved by the recipient they would not have been awarded. Two types existed: Landmine Clearance (army), Mine Clearance (navy). Both were issued as pendants suspended from a medal ribbon. The navy version came in three types: early, gilt and enamel; intermediate, painted brass; later, painted aluminium. Of these three types the latter is the most common while the other two are significantly rarer. Unusually for the Soviet Army and Navy, it is the Army Landmine Clearance badge which is the rarest type to be found. The Navy Mine Clearance badge was issued from the 1960s onwards. Presumably the army version originated at the same time, but in this author's experience only the painted aluminium version has been encountered (suggesting a shorter date range). Also unusual for Soviet badges, the Army Landmine Clearance badges were lacquered – a feature shared with only a small number of other badges (for example, late issue Suvorov Graduation badges and Komsomol Distinction in Military Service award).

Left to right: all later type Combat Mine Clearance Army, Excellence in Cultural Achievement, Combat Mine Clearance Navy.

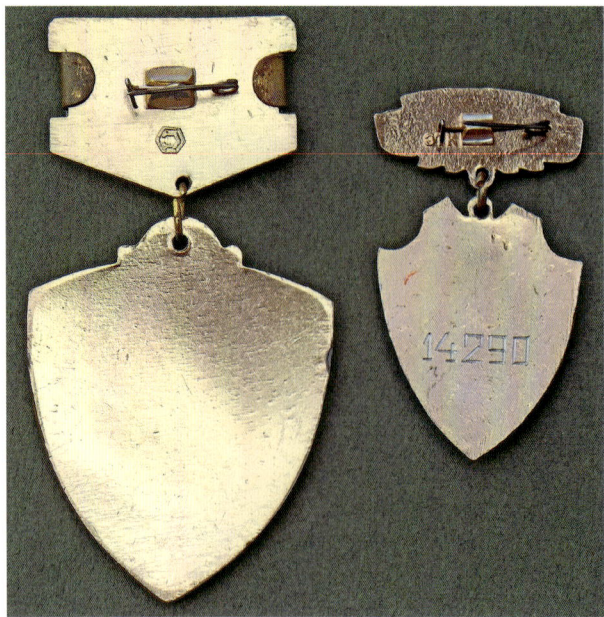

Reverse, left to right, Combat Mine Clearance, Excellence in Cultural Achievement.

Youth Membership Pins

The Soviet government sought to control every aspect of a citizen's life in order to ensure their work, loyalty and devotion to the State. Political education, therefore, could never start too young and many Soviet youths joined the KOMSOMOL (All-Union Leninist Young Communist League). Membership was rewarded with a small badge, which was worn on the uniforms of all ranks (unlike sports badges, which were worn only by ranks below that of field officer). The wearing of the badge was an important statement as it advertised a certain degree of political knowledge and reliability above that of the average soldier. First instituted in 1945, the Type One Komsomol badge was a small red flag within which was contained the organisation's Cyrillic initials. This badge was made of gilt brass and enamel and, although not rare, is noticeably scarcer than the Type Two Komsomol badges. The Type Two Komsomol badge was again a red flag featuring the organisation's initials, but added to that was a side-profile portrait of Lenin. This design remained until 1991 and came in two basic versions: early, gilt brass and enamel; later, gilt brass with enamel-effect plastic. The latter type came in two forms: civilian pin back, and slightly larger military screw post designs (earlier types appear to have been fitted solely with a pin attachment). Further to the above mentioned badges, other variations were produced in response to landmark anniversaries, competitions (for example, the 1970 Lenin Test), and patriotic campaigns such as 'Shock Workers' (members who had lent their services to industry). The quality varied according to the date of issue with those produced after *c.* 1964 being rendered in painted aluminium.

First Type Komsomol youth pin.

Second Type Komsomol youth pin, early gilt and enamel variety.

Reverse Komsomol badges, left to right: first issue, second issue gilt and enamel.

Additional Komsomol membership pins including, centre, Komsomol Distinction in Military Service 1988–91.

Above: Soviet naval infantryman photographed after 1969 wearing the Second Type Komsomol youth pin.

Right: Bulgarian officer cadet receiving training in a Soviet military academy. He wears a range of Bulgarian badges including a pin for the Bulgarian Youth Association.

Two military awards were also issued by the Komsomol: Award for Military Valour (1960s–1991), Distinction in Military Service (1988–91). The Award for Military Valour was a multiple construction made of gold and silver gilt and enamel, whereas the Distinction in Military Service (reflecting the dire economic state of the USSR during its closing years) was significantly more modest in size and construction – painted and lacquered aluminium. Both awards, however, are quite scarce and equally collectable.

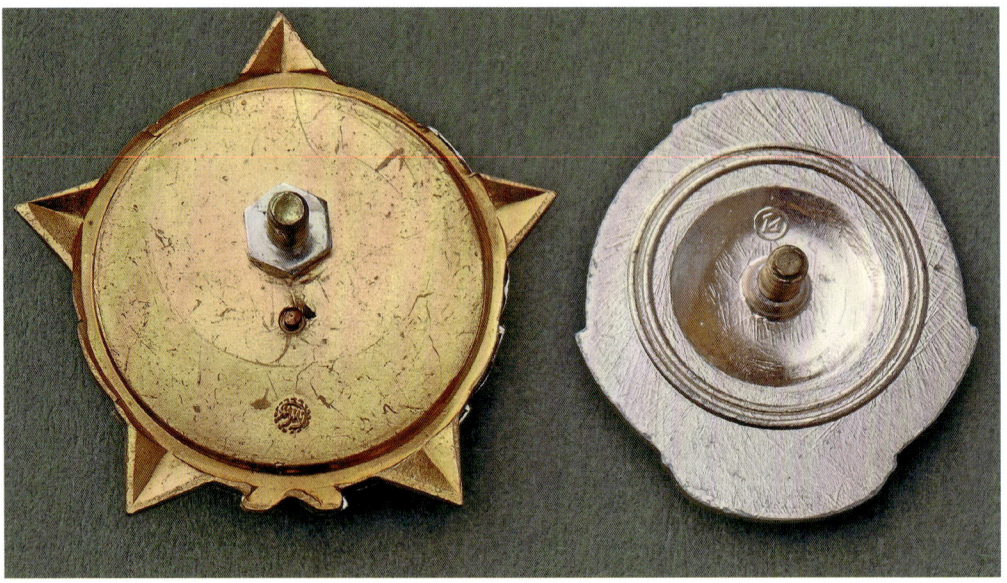

Komsomol badge of Military Valour (1960s–'80s).

Reverse, left to right: Komsomol badge of Military Valour, Komsomol Distinction in Military Service.

Guards Badges

The Guards badge (first instituted in 1943) was a distinction given to units that had distinguished themselves in battle. Once awarded, the Guards status was conferred upon every new man who had the honour to join the unit. The badge itself was a gilt wreath and red banner advertising the legend GUARD in Cyrillic characters. As well as the soldier's uniform, the guard insignia also appeared on the banners and vehicles of the division. One might argue that it was an award easily won for those who had come after the fight, but being part of a Guards division carried a number of high expectations. A Guardsman was expected to train harder and fight with greater vigour than the average soldier. In times of war, the Guards divisions were always expected to lead the army and so enter battle first (particularly at those points along the battle front which presented the greatest danger/challenge).

Second World War era Guards badges, left to right: early and later.

Reverse of Second World War Type Guards badges.

Guards badges, left to right: 1949 Type and 1960s painted aluminium.

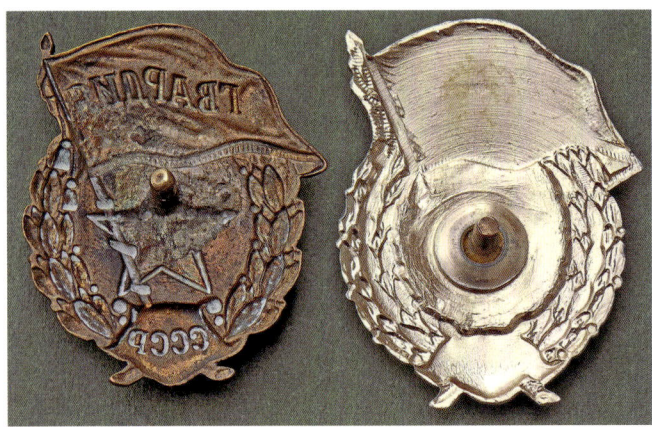

Reverse Guards badges, left to right: 1949 Type and 1960s painted aluminium.

The first Guards badge to fall within the range of this study was the 1949 Type. It offered a slight departure from earlier designs in that it was the first Guards badge to feature a fringe along the bottom of the red banner. In all other respects, the 1949 Type Guards badge was the same as its wartime predecessors. In the 1950s, however, the traditional circular shape badge gave way to an oval wreath and a more pronounced ripple effect on the banner. From there more subtle changes took place in the form of alterations to the size and shape of the lettering and an increased amount of detailing on the central star. As a whole, though, the post-war design remained largely unchanged until the 1980s when the last Soviet Guards badge was issued. The 1980s Type Guards badge was a revival of the wartime badges in that it had an oval wreath and only very subtle rippling on the banner. It is not particularly rare, but when compared to other post-war Guards badges it should be seen as scarce. Many painted aluminium Guards badges do exist, which were produced for the tourist trade (some having 'Made in the USSR' in English on the reverse) but the only official painted aluminium Guards badge was produced in the 1960s and, unlike the unofficial badges, had a screw post attachment. The quality of the 1960s painted aluminium Guards badge is significantly reduced when compared to its gilt brass and enamel contemporaries, but its comparative rarity makes it the most potentially collectable and valuable of its kind. Painted gilt brass Guards badges are encountered, but these are reproductions.

Guards Badges

Guards badges, left to right: 1950s, 1960s, 1970s.

Reverse Guards badges, left to right: 1960s and 1970s.

Guards badge, soft alloy variant of unknown date.

Replica Guards badge produced for the tourist market.

Last issue Guards badge, 1980s.

Reverse 1980s-issue Guards badge.

Soviet artillery officer photographed in 1980 wearing the 1960s painted aluminium Guards badge.

Soviet conscript photographed after 1971 wearing his Guards badge in the most commonly prescribed order of wear.

Soviet airman photographed in 1971 wearing the Guards badge in an alternative order of sequence.

Military Proficiency Badges

During the 1950s the Soviet armed forces introduced a range of Military Proficiency badges, which were destined to become some of the most prolific of all the military badges of the post-war era. They came in four grades: Third, Second, First and Master classes. The first type (one of five distinct variations) was made of high-quality gilt brass and enamel. As can be expected, the Master Class in Military Proficiency was always awarded in the smallest numbers and so is now the most collectable, with the Type One being the most collectable of them all. Unsurprisingly, therefore, the Type One Military Proficiency badges have been the subject of reproductions. The quality of these reproductions is very high, making them almost indistinguishable from the originals. What tends to give the reproductions away is the overall newness of the reverse (the forgers do not seem to care to age the reverse side as they do the obverse); a slight blurring of the reverse impression can also be observed, and a modern screw plate is often applied – one lacking in any marker's mark or writing. In the late 1950s the Type One badge was replaced by the Type Two. In many respects, the Type Two was much the same as the Type One except that the latter was made of a heavier gilt brass, and fitted with a pin attachment rather than a screw post. The star pattern within the central blue field of the Type One was removed and did not reappear until the Type Four was issued in the 1970s. Of all the Military Proficiency badges the Type Two appears to be the rarest, but has the misfortune not to survive in good condition, often being heavily tarnished.

The 1960s witnessed the introduction of the Type Three Military Proficiency badge. Still made of gilt brass, it was different to the earlier types in that the metal

Type One Military Proficiency badges, left to right: Master, classes One, Two, Three.

Second Type Military Proficiency badges.

Type Three Military Proficiency badges.

was lighter and the blue field constructed of synthetic enamel. Further to these changes more subtle differences included a resizing of the numbers, laurel leaves and red star device. Eventually, the quality of the Military Proficiency badges declined in favour of the more economical painted aluminium (1970s Type Four), which coloured the central blue field with an intensely dark-blue finish. This type was produced by a number of manufacturers and so can be found in a variety of forms indicated by differences in pin attachment, maker's marks and shades of gilt paint. The gilt paint, incidentally, fades with age and the oldest examples commonly appear silver as opposed to gold. The final example was the Type Five. This version was also constructed of painted aluminium, but had undergone a number of subtle variations compared to that of the Type Four. Principally, the star pattern was removed once more from the central blue field, a screw post became more common than a pin attachment, and the intensely dark-blue paint of the Type Four was replaced by a paler enamel-effect gloss.

Type Four Military Proficiency badges.

Type Five Military Proficiency badge.

Variations of the Type Four Military proficiency badge.

Bulgarian Military Proficiency badges.

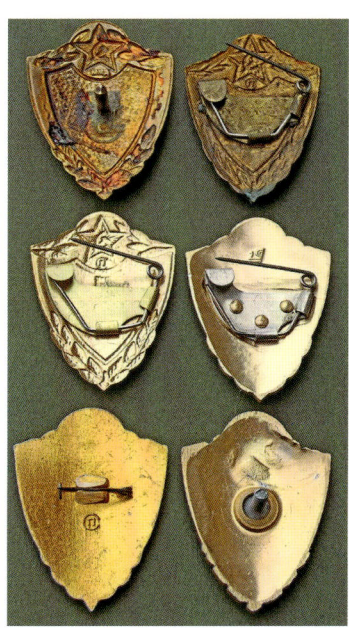

Reverse, clockwise: Type One, Two, Three, Five, Three, Four Military Proficiency badge.

Soviet signalman photographed in 1978 wearing the Type Four Military Proficiency badge. He also wears one of the dated 'Shock Worker' Komsomol pins.

Parachute Badges

Left: 1968 Type One Instructor Parachute badge recording 375 jumps.

Right: Reverse 1968 Type One Instructor Parachute badge.

The Soviet Army had been in the habit of rewarding its paratroopers for successful training and jumps since the 1930s with a design of badge that had remained little changed until 1955. In 1955 the first of the post-war parachute badges was issued. This basic qualification existed in the form of a two-piece construction. Unlike its descendants, the 1955 Type Basic Parachute Qualification badge did not accommodate a numbering system that could record the completion of further successful jumps. However, on the completion of the tenth successful jump the paratrooper qualified for the Excellent Parachute badge. Unlike the 1955 Type Basic Parachute badge, the 1955 Type Excellent Parachute badge had an earlier and later type, indicated by either a two- or one-piece construction. In addition, the Excellent Parachute badge recorded additional jumps via a pendant suspended from the base of the badge. Naturally enough, those badges which record the highest number of jumps are the most collectable.

1955 Type One Basic Parachute badge (two-piece construction).

Reverse 1955 Type One Basic Parachute badge.

Soviet paratrooper from the late 1950s to early 1960s wearing the 1955 Excellent Parachute badge.

Both 1955 Type Parachute badges were made of gilt brass and enamel. Of a higher status, but reduced quality, was the 1966 Type Parachute Instructor badge. Made of painted aluminium, this short-lived badge came in three grades: Third, Second and First class. The majority tend to have a blue field, although there is a scarcer version with a green field. It is not known whether or not the use of a green field was deliberate or accidental, considering yellow and blue make green, and so further research is required on this point. Whatever the case, the brief duration of the badge has ensured that it is amongst the rarest of the post-war parachute awards.

In 1968 all previous parachute badges were discontinued in favour of a new range of awards, which remained in service until the end of the USSR. The 1968 Type Parachute badges came in the standard three classes established by the 1955 and 1966 types: Basic, Excellent Parachute and Instructor. The difference was a refinement in the style of the badges to become lighter and slimmer in the case of the Basic and Excellent Parachute. For the Parachute Instructor, the design became more substantial in both terms of its look and construction. In all three cases, the 1968 Type Parachute badges came in two basic forms: early and later. For the Basic Parachute and Excellent Parachute badges, the difference was in the style of the aeroplane featured within its design; understandably, the later type sported an aircraft of a more modern appearance. Beyond this observation other differences can be noted as a consequence of a variety of manufacturers having produced the badge during its twenty-three-year history. Unlike the 1955 Type Parachute badges, all of the 1968 Type badges recorded the number of additional jumps. In the case of the Basic and Excellent Parachute badges the additional jumps were on a diamond pendant. The 1968 Type Excellent Parachute badge differed from the 1968 Basic Parachute and the 1955 types in that it carried a unit of ten (ten, twenty, thirty and so on) within its central field (a painted aluminium numeral attached via pins).

The 1968 Type Parachute Instructor badge was more sophisticated in that it was of a three-piece construction, whereas the other 1968 types were either single or two-piece construction. Jumps were recorded in units of 100 on the body of the badge, while

Parachute Badges

Standard 1966 Type Parachute Instructor badge, left to right: Classes One, Two, Three.

Reverse standard 1966 Parachute Instructor badge.

1966 Parachute Instructor badge rare green variant.

1968 Basic Parachute Badges, left to right: early aeroplane and later aeroplane.

Reverse 1968 Basic Parachute badges, left to right: earlier and later versions.

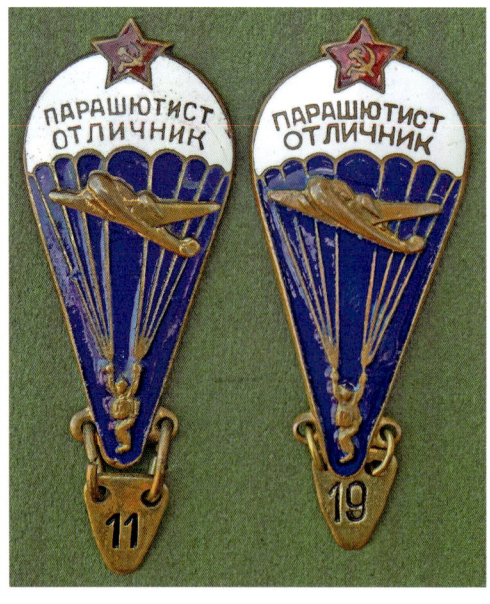

1955 Type Excellent Parachute badges, left to right: two-piece and single-piece constructions.

Parachute Badges

Reverse 1955 Excellent Parachute badges, left to right: two-piece and single construction.

1968 Type Excellent Parachute badges, left to right: earlier and later.

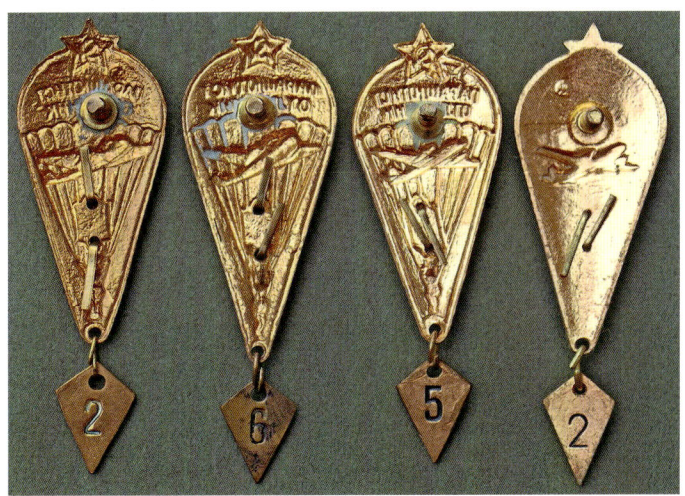

1968 Type Excellent Parachute badges, left to right: early and later examples plus variations in manufacturer.

Variant 1968 Type Excellent Parachute badges, left to right: painted aluminium and gloss painted brass.

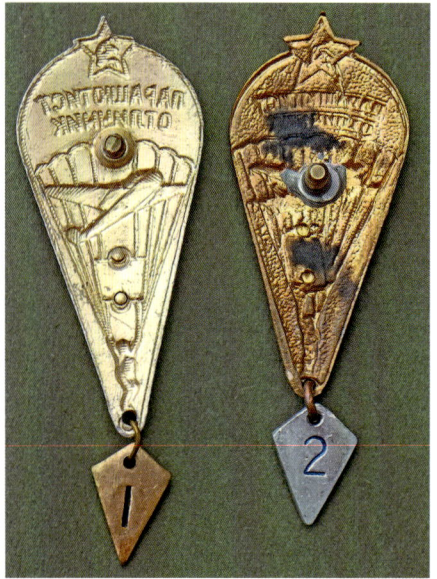

Reverse variant 1968 Type Excellent Parachute badge, left to right: painted aluminium and gloss painted brass.

additional numbering was supplied via a pendant suspended below the badge (starting with ten and rising in units of fifteen). The early versions sported, by then, a vintage aircraft, while the later designs had an aircraft of more modern design. Differences were also observed as a result of variations in the size of the numbers and lettering due to a variety of manufacturers. Later changes included the introduction of a one-piece construction in the 1980s (the numbering of which started at 100 and went all the way through to 1,000 jumps). The numbers quoted seem inconceivable, but it is worth noting that the Soviet armed forces made extensive use of simulators and so many of the jumps would have been simulated (making the accumulation of very high numbers quite realistic).

1968 Type Parachute Instructor badges, left to right: early two-piece and later single construction.

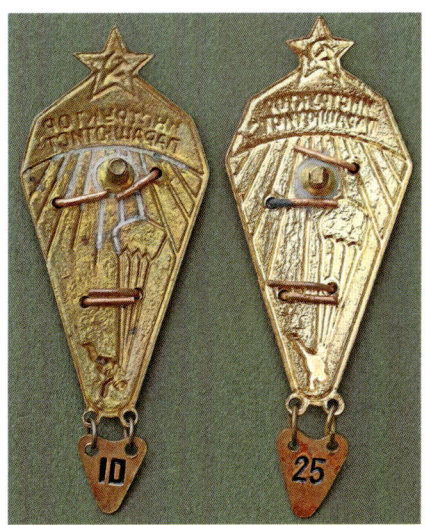

Reverse 1968 Parachute Instructor badges, left to right: early and later.

1968 Type Parachute Instructor badges, left to right: last issue, painted variants.

Reverse 1968 Type Parachute Instructor badge, left to right: last issue and painted variant.

Bulgarian Parachute badge.

Extended Service Clasps

The average conscript served two years in the army and air force and three years in the navy and rocket defence. For many Soviet men conscription was an unwelcome chore, but some did find that they liked military life and so continued their service beyond the period of conscription. This extended service was celebrated through the awarding of the Extended Service clasp. Such awards were instituted in 1957 with each of the three main services adopting its own design (in short, a badge featuring the individual service's flag). The exact number of additional years served was recorded by a pendant suspended from the badge by brass links. Most Extended Service clasps record one or two years' additional service, but a few rarer examples do reach double figures.

In keeping with the tradition established by other Soviet badges of the post-war era, the Extended Service clasps came in two basic types: early and later. The earlier clasps were a combination of painted gilt brass and enamel, while the later badges were constructed of painted aluminium. Within these two types variations existed as a result of different manufacturers having produced the badge (usually indicated by the maker's mark). The overall design and dimensions remained the same, with the exceptions that the central star and wreath can differ in terms of the size and height of their profiles. Additionally, the hammer and sickle device can be of a different size. The later type Extended Service clasps are more common than their predecessors,

Soviet warrant officer (and veteran of the Great Patriotic War) serving in a tank division wearing the First Type Army Extended Service clasp.

although the prices do not vary hugely. Army and air force clasps are found more often than those issued by the navy, but that is not to say that the navy version is particularly rare or even scarce – just not encountered as often. The author is yet to encounter an Extended Service clasp with a screw attachment so the assumption is that all such clasps had a pin. This observation can make the locating of the maker's marks difficult as such maker's marks can commonly be obscured by the pin attachment.

Above left: Early Type Army Extended Service clasps.

Above right: Reverse First Type Army Extended Service clasp.

Left: First Type Extended Service clasp, top to bottom: air force, navy.

Extended Service Clasps 51

Left: Reverse First Type Extended Service clasps for air force and navy.

Right: Second Type Extended Service clasp, top to bottom: navy, army.

Left: Second Type Extended Service clasp, air force.

Right: Reverse Second Type Extended Service clasp, air force.

Officer Academy Graduation Badges

Suvorov and Nakhimov Schools

The first graduation badge a future Soviet officer could have been awarded during the Cold War era was either a Suvorov (army and air force) or Nakhimov (navy) Graduation badge, which advertised attendance at one of the USSR's military prep schools. The design of each of the two badges changed little over time and, largely speaking, only did change in order to accommodate a cheaper method or quality of construction. The most common form of attachment was a screw post, but the 1960s did witness the use of a pin. These badges have been subject to reproductions, the most common of which are those that have had a name plate pertaining to a specific school applied to them. Such badges did exist, but they are very rare and date from the 1940s. Reproductions often conflict with the originals by being a one-piece construction. The last point to note about the reproductions is that they frequently feature the wrong portrait of Suvorov – the originals showing only the head and neck, while the fakes include the head, neck, and shoulders.

Soviet Military Prep-School Graduation badges, left to right: 1960s, 1970s–1991, 1980s navy.

Reverse Prep-School Graduation badges, left to right: 1960s, 1970s-91, 1980s navy.

Military Schools

For many Soviet officers their first piece of formal training came from one of the specialist training schools. These institutions also rewarded their graduates with a badge, although the appearance was altered several times before settling for a single, unified design. The First Type Military School Graduation badges were issued *c.* 1946. The central device, contained within an oval wreath, featured the branch of service insignia of the awarding school. Beneath was a plaque recording graduation year, a separate piece attached via brass pins. This design was discontinued in 1955 when the one-piece construction Type Two was introduced. It did not advertise the year of graduation but instead featured the Cyrillic initials of the USSR. In turn, the Type Two was replaced in 1958 by the Type Three Military School Graduation badge. The Type Three was a unified design issued by all military schools and remained in service until 1991. As a consequence, the Type Three Military School Graduation badge is fairly common. Due to the shorter duration of the Types One and Two Graduation badges, the surviving examples are significantly rarer and so more sought after. The branch of service and year can also have an impact upon the badge's rarity and value, with the older years generally being considered more valuable. As a whole, the graduation badges from the combat arms (such as tank or paratrooper schools) tend to be more desirable, although the rarest in terms of the numbers issued is from one of the support services: Fuel & Lubricant Supply School. All types of this class of badge have been heavily reproduced, usually identified by their reduced quality. In the case of the Type One Military School badges, reproductions come as a single-piece construction rather than the correct two-piece construction.

Military School Graduation badges, left to right: First Type, Third Type.

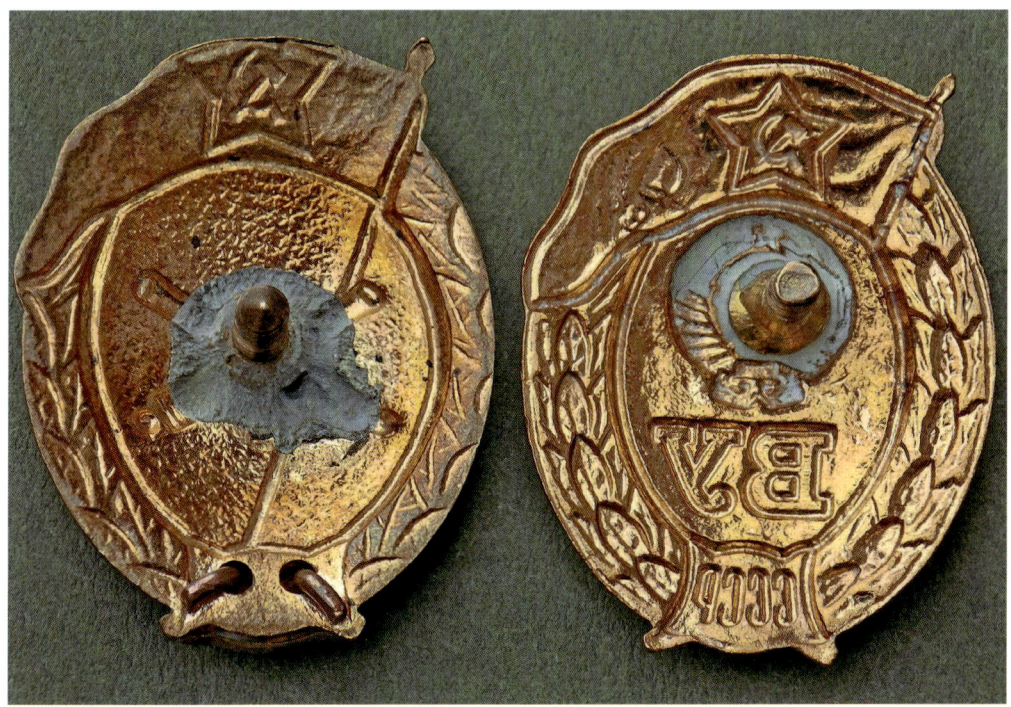

Reverse Military School Graduation badges, left to right: First Type, Third Type.

Military Colleges

The next step up from the military school was the military college. The first badges issued by these institutions that were distinct from the higher academies came in the form of the Type One instituted in 1961. Made of high-quality gilt brass and enamel, it was a gold rhombus containing a blue field. Within the blue field was the Soviet coat of arms as well as the hammer and sickle device. (The reverse side features three rivets which hold the aforementioned insignia to the body of the badge, a feature not seen on reproductions.) This was replaced by the Type Two in 1982. In contrast to the Type One, the Type Two was silver gilt and featured a blue field that contained only the Soviet coat of arms. The reverse featured a single retaining rivet and maker's mark. Neither badge happens to be particularly rare, although their status as graduation badges means that they have been subject to reproduction. When this has happened the badge is usually of a one-piece rather than a two- or three-piece construction, or is of significantly inferior materials which are not attached via the rivet method employed on the originals.

Technical College Graduation badge, left to right: First Type military, civil engineering college; Second Type military.

Military Colleges

Above: Reverse Technical College Graduation badges, left to right: First Type, Second Type.

Right: Soviet tank officer photographed in 1989 wearing the Type One Military College Graduation badge. He also wears the Combined Services clasp, Second Class.

Higher Academies

For most officers their formal training would conclude with attendance at one of the Soviet armed force's higher academies. These higher academies issued graduation badges from before the timeframe of this book, but the examples that concern this study started with the Type One Higher Academy Graduation badge instituted in 1950. The Type One was a solid silver rhombus with a white field. The design included a detailed Soviet coat of arms and a nameplate advertising the name of the awarding institution. It was a three-piece construction with the coat of arms and nameplate attached via silver pins. In 1954 the Type Two was introduced. It differed from the Type One in that its coat of arms was attached to the badge via a rivet rather than silver pins (making it more robust and secure). As with the military schools, the value of the Type One and Type Two Higher Academy Graduation badges depends on the name and/or branch of service of the awarding institution especially when it is considered that some were general academies for the very highest ranking officers. In 1957 the Type Two was replaced by the Type Three Higher Academy Graduation badge. This design was the first of the unified badges, and so did without the individual nameplate. The quality remained the same, though, and the Type Three continued to be made of silver until 1960. In 1960 the final Type Four Higher Academy Graduation badge was introduced. It was constructed to the same standard, but was made of alloy instead of silver. This badge remained in service until the end of the USSR. With the nameplate having been removed, general academies started producing their own distinct badge which was a suitable gold (as opposed to silver) colour – the quality of which is always very high. Reproductions of all types exist and are identifiable by virtue of their overall newness or poor quality construction. A good indication is the thickness of the coat of arms and red star. An original will have a finely detailed coat of arms with a high relief, while the enamelled star is quite thick and very securely fixed to the badge. Reproductions tend to be slimmer and looser fitting. On rare occasions a Soviet officer would have previously graduated from a civilian academy prior to military service. This seems to have happened to officers with an engineering degree and so they wore a civilian academy badge on their uniforms (note accompanying archive photograph), but not exclusively. Some university graduates chose not to be career soldiers and completed a period of conscription as a regular soldier instead, meaning that civilian graduation badges can also be found on the uniforms of other ranks as well as officers. Many of the Warsaw Pact nations copied Soviet designs and photographs of badges from other nations have been included to help the reader avoid confusion.

Higher Academy Graduation badges, left to right: 1954 Type and 1960.

Reverse Higher Academy Graduation badges, left to right: 1954 Type, 1960 Type.

Bulgarian Higher Academy Graduation badge.

Left: Hungarian Military College Graduation badge.

Right: Hungarian Higher Academy Graduation badge.

Left: Polish Higher Academy Graduation badge.

Right: Czechoslovak Higher Academy Graduation badge.

Soviet artillery officer wearing one of the named Higher Academy Graduation badges. He also wears a Suvorov badge awarded by a military prep-school, Anti-Aircraft Troops of the Country badge, and the prestigious Order of Service to Motherland in the Armed Forces of the USSR.

Soviet Navy officer wearing one of the unified Higher Academy Graduation badges. He also wears a Soviet Navy badge celebrating the completion of a long voyage.

Left: Soviet Officer photographed in 1951 wearing one of the pre-1950 graduation badges.

Below: Unnamed Soviet general wearing the unified General Academy Graduation badge.

Soviet Air Force officer photographed in 1976 wearing a civilian engineering academy graduation badge. He also wears the smaller Second Type Flight Engineers clasp.

Technical Clasps

Air Force Clasps

Soviet officers were not eligible for the Extended Service clasps, but could often qualify for one of several technical clasps. For the greater part, these clasps were the preserve of the air force (a reflection of the fact that it was a highly mechanised force) with only a small number issued by the army and navy.

Ground-based air force technicians could either qualify for the Combined Services clasp (mentioned below) or the Flight Engineer clasp. The latter clasp was instituted in 1948 and appears to have only come in an unclassified type (no system of numbering or grading having been employed). The Type One Flight Engineer clasp was issued until 1958 and was a large-sized badge made from hollow stamped silver gilt brass and enamel with a pin attachment. The metal was thin but strong, meaning that most surviving examples are to be found in good condition. It was replaced by the smaller Type Two, which was replaced itself in the 1970s by a solid-cast version made of painted aluminium.

For aircrews two types of clasp existed, those for pilots and navigators. For the purposes of this study, the Pilot and Navigator Proficiency clasps started with the Type One instituted in 1950. Both versions came in four classes: First, Second, Third, Unclassified, which remained until 1961. The Pilot Proficiency clasp featured a central shield, which was colour coded according to the class: gold, First Class; silver, Second Class; blue enamel, Third Class. Navigator Proficiency clasps featured a conventional bomb as its central device, again colour coded as before. Between 1961 and 1966 it is not entirely certain what happened. It is commonly believed that the replacement Pilot and Navigator clasps were instituted in 1966, but photographic evidence has convinced this author that the 1966 Type clasps were introduced as early as 1961. Whatever the actual case may have been, the 1961/66 Type Pilot and Navigator clasps remained in service until 1991. The majority were gilt brass and enamel with silver highlights, although some less common examples are found in painted aluminium. This latter type should be approached with caution as it is not generally recognised that these clasps were ever produced in painted aluminium. In 1971 a fifth class was added to the Pilot and Navigator Proficiency clasps, that of Sniper. They are quite common, although the Navigator Sniper is a little less commonplace than the pilot's version. In both cases the early types have a noticeably larger star than the later versions. Of an unknown type is a badge what appears to have been a Unified Sniper clasp. Made of painted aluminium and attached via a screw post rather than the more standard pin there is little that can be said about this badge other than the observation that it has, thus far, failed to provide any supporting documentation. As with other painted aluminium air force clasps, this clasp is probably best viewed with suspicion. A badge that was never issued, but is certainly authentic is the clasp intended for the pilots of aircraft stationed on board navy carriers. It was authorised in 1991, but was not manufactured until 1992 and so went unissued. It survives in good numbers and in good condition (partly due to its high-quality) and is it is not at all rare, but may well be one to watch and could become collectable as time goes on.

Flight Engineer clasps, top to bottom: early and later types.

Reverse Flight Engineer clasps, top to bottom: first issue, last issue painted aluminium.

Unclassified Pilot clasps, top to bottom: 1950 Hungarian version and 1950 Soviet issue.

Navigator clasps, top to bottom: Soviet Class One, Hungarian issue.

Technical Clasps

Above: Pilot clasps, top to bottom: 1960s Hungarian version, Soviet Class One.

Right: Reverse Soviet clasps, top to bottom: Pilot, Navigator, Pilot.

Above: 1950s Pilot clasps Third Class.

Left: 1961 Pilot clasps, top to bottom: Class One, Two, Three.

1961 Navigator clasps, top to bottom: Class One, Two, Three.

1971 Sniper Class clasps, top to bottom: Pilot, Navigator, Undesignated.

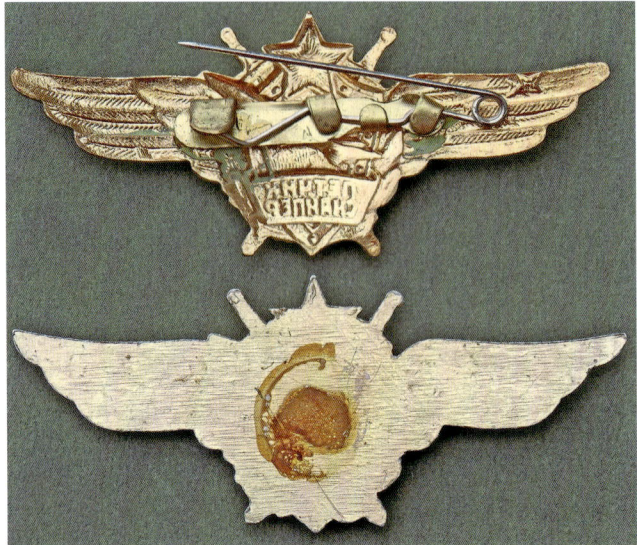

Reverse Sniper Class clasps, top to bottom: Pilot, Undesignated.

Top to bottom: Aircraft Carrier Flight Crew, Unclassified Pilots clasp.

1961 Navigator clasps painted aluminium version.

Technical Clasps

Reverse, top to bottom: Aircraft Carrier Air Crew, Signals, Navigator clasp later painted aluminium.

Hero of the Soviet Union, and pioneering cosmonaut, Yuri Gagarin photographed in 1961. This postcard shows the Soviet airman wearing the Pilot Clasp, First Class, often designated as Model 1966.

Soviet Air Force officer from the early to mid-1950s wearing the 1948 Flight Engineer clasp.

Soviet pilot officer photographed in 1953 wearing the 1950 Type Pilot Clasp, Third Class. He also wears a pre-1950 graduation badge issued by a Soviet military flight school.

Soviet Air Force officer photographed in 1953 wearing the earlier, large-size Pilot Clasp.

Technical Clasps 73

Soviet Air Force officer photographed in the 1950s wearing the 1950 Type Unclassified Pilot Clasp.

Soviet Air Force officer photographed in 1951 wearing a pre-1950 Type Navigator Clasp.

Soviet Air Force officer and pioneer cosmonaut wearing the Type 1961/66 Pilot Clasp, Second Class.

Army Clasps

In regards to the army three clasps were available: Signals, Tankers and Combined Services. Of these, the trade specific badges for signalmen and tankers were issued from the mid-1950s until 1961. They came in four grades: Third, Second, First and Master class. The Tank Proficiency clasp came with a screw post attachment (those fitted with a pin were of Hungarian manufacture, which was of a less sophisticated design than the Soviet-made pins). The Signals Proficiency clasp came as either a hollow stamped or solid backed version. Both were fitted with a pin. In each case, these badges were constructed of gilt brass and enamel – at no time painted aluminium. The Combined Services clasp replaced all previous clasps. As with its predecessors, the Combined Services clasp came in the same four grades. Like the Tank Proficiency clasp before it, the Combined Services clasp was constructed from a mixture of gilt brass, enamel, silver gilt wash and black painted highlights. Uncommonly, the Combined Services clasp was shared with the air force (most commonly anti-aircraft troops). Some painted aluminium examples have been found, but it is not yet clear how authentic they are. Certainly there is no shortage of the more expensively produced gilt and enamel badges so it is not likely that a cheaper version was required.

Above: Tank Proficiency clasp, Master Class.

Left: Tank Proficiency clasps, top to bottom: First, Second, Third classes.

Technical Clasps

Reverse Tank Proficiency clasps, top to bottom: Soviet, Hungarian.

Signals Proficiency clasp, Second Class.

Combined Services clasp, Master Class.

Left: Combined Services clasps, top to bottom: Class One, Two, Three.

Below: Reverse Combined Services clasps.

Above: Reverse Combined Services clasp painted aluminium version.

Right: Soviet Air Force officer photographed c. 1975–1991 wearing the Combined Services Clasp, Third Class. He also wears the 1960 Unified Higher Academy Graduation badge as well as the Anti-Aircraft Troops of the Country award.

Navy Clasps

There are only two naval clasps to speak of, those awarded to commanders of surface craft and submarines. In both cases, each badge came in only two grades: silver and gold. The early versions were made of silver, but gave way in the 1960s to gilt brass and then in the 1970s to silver and gold-coloured alloy. Those that predate the 1960s are of particularly good quality and should be considered as being quite rare. The later versions are more common, although they have not been free of reproductions and most of the examples one would encounter are fake. The best indications of an original are a maker's mark to the reverse of the badge, construction from sturdy materials, and a screw plate with a maker's mark.

Navy clasps, top to bottom: Surface Craft Gold Class, Submarine Silver Class.

Navy clasps, top to bottom: Surface Craft, Submarine.

Celebration Badges

The USSR was never one to miss an opportunity to celebrate an anniversary, particularly those of a military nature, and Soviet celebration badges could easily fill a book of their own. For the purposes of this study, it will be enough to draw the reader's attention to the various categories that existed and illustrate them with a few meaningful examples. The reason for this is because many of the celebration badges produced by the Soviet armed forces were issued to a soldier at the end of, or after, his period of service and so do not quite match the true focus of this book. To miss them out completely, however, would be to miss a truly pleasing visual spectacle, and so here some of them are presented to the reader. Of the type to have been worn on the uniforms of active service personnel, the most interesting and collectable of all needs to have been those issued by training schools. Usually such badges celebrated a landmark anniversary and were only issued during the course of a single year (making all such examples quite rare). No one design was adopted and, although the vast majority were a rhombus in shape, the designs are all quite unique. As can be expected, this class of badge has been subject to significant reproduction, the general indications of which are a single-piece construction as opposed to multiple pieces and an unnamed screw plate.

Soviet Naval School thirtieth anniversary badge.

Warsaw Pact

This category of badge includes the rare number of foreign badges that made it onto any Soviet uniform. The Warsaw Pact (an agreement on friendship, co-operation and mutual assistance) was the Soviet version of NATO. In truth, it gave the USSR the excuse to permanently station troops within the borders of neighbouring countries. Part of the pact on co-operation was to take participate in military war-games. These usually involved the USSR and at least one other pact nation, although all-party war-games were held every few years. Whatever the case, the games were concluded with the issuing of a celebratory badge (manufactured by the host nation). As a result of the latter point, the design and quality of these celebration badges varies hugely (although they are readily identified by virtue of the fact they always feature the flags of the participating nations, titles in the form of shield, brother-in-arms, or the specific place name where the games were held, and a date). The remaining class of Warsaw Pact badge to mention were those celebrating the landmark anniversaries of twenty-five, thirty and thirty-five years. All of these badges were manufactured in the USSR and made of painted and lacquered brass.

Similar to the Warsaw Pact anniversary badges, the USSR produced the Good Memory of the Soviet Armed Forces badges. For the most part they were given to foreign guests who had observed a war-games exercise. These badges originated in the 1960s (of which two known examples exist) and were initially made of gilt brass and enamels until the mid-1970s when the manufacture went over to painted aluminium. All examples are scarce, but those from the 1960s are the rarest and so most collectable.

Warsaw Pact celebration badges, top left to bottom right: Hungary, East Germany, Hungary, Bulgaria.

Above: Czechoslovak Warsaw Pact celebration badges.

Right: Early 1970s issue Good Memory of the Soviet Armed Forces badge.

Later issue Good Memory of the Soviet Armed Forces badge.

Navy Celebration Badges

By far the most common celebration badge produced by the USSR was its extensive range of naval celebration badges. These came in two forms: veteran badges, and those celebrating the completion of a long voyage. Like the Training School Anniversary badges, the Navy Celebration badges came in an innumerable number of designs. Many of the veteran badges followed a similar design by copying the type established by the Long Voyage badges, but even many more produced their own design and so the range and variety is quite staggering. Unlike the training school anniversary badges, though, the veteran badges do not appear to have had a limited run and many long-serving vessels seem to have issued the same badge year on year. As a consequence, although many of the badges pertain to a named vessel they are still relatively common and so not as collectable as one might have been tempted to think.

The history of the Long Voyage badge started in 1956 when the Soviet Navy issued a commemorative badge to celebrate its visit to the United Kingdom that same year. It set the template of the Long Voyage badge design which, with some slight variation, is still in use with the Russian Navy today. The Standard Type Long Voyage badges were instituted in the 1960s with different designs for the crew members of surface craft and submarines. These first-issue badges were constructed of gilt brass, enamel and silver highlights, with a pin attachment to the rear. The design and quality remained the same into the 1970s, although the pin attachment was replaced by a screw post and the quality did eventually give way and change from hot enamel to gloss paint. Curiously, the 1980s witnessed a brief resurgence of quality with the issuing of an alternative version of the gilt brass and enamel Long Voyage badge. In a separation from the past, however, the usually red features of the badge were orange in colour and the reverse had a smooth, concave finish. The manufacturer of both badges appears to have been the same, although one was fitted with a pin and the other a screw post.

Badge celebrating participation in naval wargames.

Reverse navy wargames participant's badge.

Soviet Navy Veteran badges.

Surface craft thirtieth anniversary celebration badge.

First Type Long Voyage badge for surface craft.

1970s–1991 Long Voyage badge surface craft.

Celebration Badges

1980s issue Long Voyage surface craft.

Reverse Long Voyage badge surface craft, top to bottom: first issue, 1980s, 1970s.

Long Voyage badge submarine, left to right: first issue, second issue.

Above: Long Voyage submarine 1980s issue.

Left: Reverse Long Voyage submarine, top to bottom: first issue, 1980s, 1970s.

Soviet sailor photographed in 1966 wearing the Soviet Navy Long Voyage badge.

Soviet paratrooper photographed in the mid-1960s wearing a large commemorative badge issued by a Soviet Parachute School.

Often cited as being from 1976–91 was a completely different style of Long Voyage badge, which many claim were awarded to the crews of nuclear submarines and surface craft. The truth of this claim is not known, but photographic evidence has proven these badges to have been authentic. Unlike other Long Voyage badges, the 1976 Type was of a large-size and produced only in painted aluminium. They were made by a variety of manufacturers (four to the author's knowledge) and so often demonstrate subtle differences to the obverse and reverse sides. These differences included the use of matt or gloss paints, alterations in the size of the lettering, and both pin and screw post attachments. Collectively they are not at all rare and so fail to generate much interest with collectors.

Long Voyage painted aluminium variant.

Reverse Long Voyage painted aluminium badges with screw post and pin attachments.

Miscellaneous Military Badges

This last section deals with a small number of badges that do not really fit into any other category. The most prestigious badge found within this eclectic mix was not in fact a military badge, but it is mentioned because it was frequently featured on the uniforms of high-ranking military personnel. It was the Supreme Soviet Member's badge and denoted membership of the joint highest authority within the USSR. Each of the Soviet Republics had its own version, which was based on that region's national flag. The attachment could be via screw post or a pin, but the quality of manufacture was always consistently good with each example being inscribed with its own serial number. Of all the Soviet political awards, it is one of the most collectable.

Left: Soviet cosmonaut wearing the Ukrainian Socialist Republic's version of the Supreme Soviet Members' badge.

Right: Soviet officer from a civil authority wearing the Russian Socialist Republic's version of the Supreme Soviet Members' badge.

In 1975 the Soviet Air Force introduced the Anti-Aircraft Troops of the Nation badge, which was awarded to air defence personnel including interceptor pilots. The badge came in an early and later type, although the overall design remained unchanged. The early type was made of gilt brass and enamel, while the later type was painted aluminium. Uncommon to painted aluminium badges, though, the later type Anti-Aircraft Troops of the Nation badge was still a two-piece construction the same as the earlier type (although the later type was secured using rivets rather than brass pins).

The final badge to mention was that given to Military Transport Police assigned traffic duties. An enormous-sized badge, it was a form of insignia rather than an award. However, the reason that it is mentioned here is because it closely resembled Soviet awards and so is sometimes mistaken as such. In its standard form it is not at all rare, although a version issued to Military Rail Transport Police is scarce (recognisable by virtue of its larger inscription). These duty badges were not confined to the military police alone and the internal army and factory guards also wore duty badges of similar design (different in that the former had a red field and the latter a green field accompanied by insignia unique to their respective organisations).

Anti-Aircraft Troops of the Country badges, left to right: standard issue, painted aluminium version.

Reverse Anti-Aircraft Troops of the Country, left to right: standard issue, painted aluminium.

Military Police Duty badge.

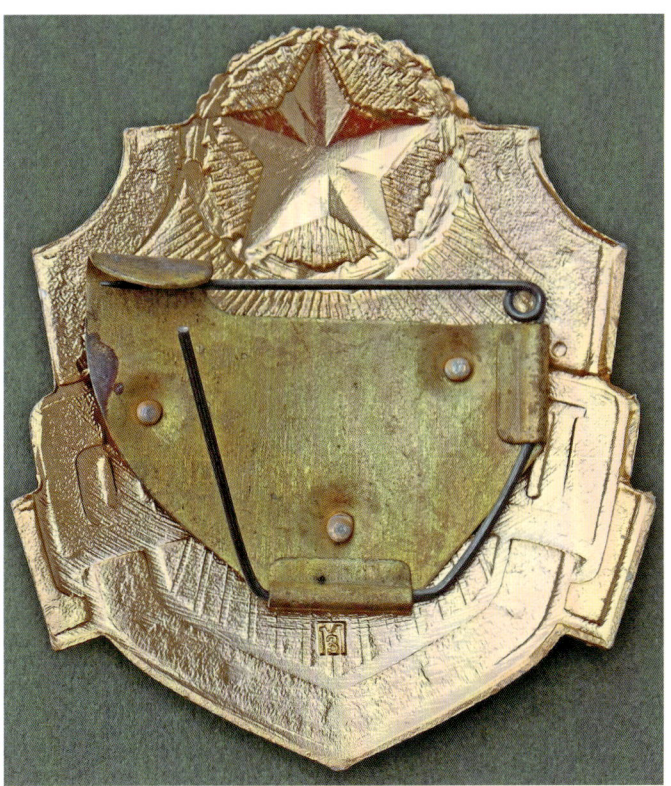

Reverse Military Police Duty badge.

Note About the Prescribed Order of Wear

As mentioned in the introduction, a word is going to be given over to the prescribed order of wear. The purpose of doing so is to give the reader a sense of the badges' value in relation to other awards as well as allow for the recognition of bogus couplings. The first thing that the reader will have noticed is that there were a lot of shared badges between the services, but not so many badges shared between the officers and men. Two basic rules to understand are that military graduation badges were issued to officers only, as were clasps with the exception of the Extended Service clasp (which was issued to other ranks, NCOs and warrant officers). Naval Long Voyage badges and Parachute badges were shared between all ranks (except Instructor badges, which appear to have remained the preserve of officers). Towards the end of the Soviet era it was not uncommon for Naval Infantry to have undergone parachute training.

Most of the badges featured were positioned on the wearer's right-hand side (third button down on closed-neck tunics, and just above the first button on open-necked tunics). Combat badges, and then awards with a pendant along with clasps, occupied the top-most portion of the tunic. Other badges were arranged parallel to the tunic buttons. The prescribed order of precedence worked from the viewer's right to left. The row of badges never appears to have exceeded four in total. If the soldier in question had more than four awards then a new line was formed below. The Guards badge took precedence, followed by Excellence, then Proficiency, Parachute/Long Voyage, Military Sport and finally Civilian Sport pins. Officer uniforms observed the following order: Guards badge, Graduation, Suvorov/Nakhimov, Anti-Aircraft Troops of the Nation, Parachute/Long Voyage. To the benefit of the forger, it will be noted from archive photographs that the order of precedence was not always strictly adhered to. In these cases the badges may appear in the wrong order, but what can also be noticed is that an officer or man will never have been wearing an award that he was not entitled to.

Note About the Prescribed Order of Wear

Above: Soviet officer awards in prescribed order of wear.

Right: Soviet officer awards in prescribed order of wear.

Above: Soviet officer awards in prescribed order of wear.

Left: Soviet Other Ranks' awards in prescribed order of wear.

Note About the Prescribed Order of Wear

Above: Soviet Other Ranks' awards in prescribed order of wear.

Right: Soviet Other Ranks' awards in prescribed order of wear.

Soviet screw plates.